The
SUPER SMART
PLANET
EARTH
Activity
Book

By Gemma Barder

Illustrated by
Isabel Muñoz

ARCTURUS

ARCTURUS

This edition published in 2023 by Arcturus Publishing Limited
26/27 Bickels Yard, 151–153 Bermondsey Street,
London SE1 3HA

Author: Gemma Barder
Illustrator: Isabel Muñoz
Editors: Becca Clunes and Lucy Doncaster
Design: Fountain Creative
Design Manager: Jessica Holliland
Managing Editor: Joe Harris

ISBN: 978-1-3988-2562-8
CH010451NT
Supplier 29, Date 0123, PI 00000708

Printed in China

What is STEM?

STEM is a world-wide initiative that aims to cultivate an interest in
Science, Technology, Engineering, and Mathematics, in an effort to
promote these disciplines to as wide a variety of students as possible.

IT'S A WONDERFUL WORLD!

From rivers and forests to mountains and oceans, this fact-packed book will take you on an incredible adventure around the planet. As you solve the puzzles and activities, you will learn more about the plants, animals, and habitats that make our amazing world!

Did you know?

Earth is more than 4.5 billion years old! Since life first appeared about 3.7 billion years ago, many different types of animals and plants have existed, from dinosaurs to donkeys. Today, it is home to an estimated trillion types of living thing—that's really quite something!

Earth is the third planet from the Sun, and is the only known planet where conditions are ideal for life.

NORTHERN FORESTS

Coniferous forests are found across northern parts of Asia, Europe, and America. These regions have long, cold winters, plenty of rainfall, and a short growing season. Circle every other letter to find the four trees that are most common in these forests. The first one has been done for you.

m s o p o r s u e c b e a p t i s n h e a l r a e r b c e h a f r i s r

S	

Many conifers have needles instead of leaves, and are called "evergreens" because they stay green all year.

A lot of birds migrate to these forests in summer to feed on the vast numbers of insects that are found there.

SPIDER MONKEY MEAL

Spider monkeys live in tropical forests and love to eat fruit.
How many mangoes can you see in this lucky monkey's pile?

Spider monkeys are so named because they look a bit like spiders when they hang by their tails with their limbs dangling.

Unlike most monkeys, spider monkeys only have very short thumbs. They curl their long fingers around branches to grip them.

PERFECT PLACE FOR A NEST

Nests can be made in lots of different places, from a hole in a tree to a remote clifftop. Follow the line from each nest to discover which one belongs to the toucan!

Toucans lay between two and four eggs at a time. They have small beaks when they are first born, which develop as the birds grow.

BRIGHT FLIGHT

Scarlet macaws are known for their bright feathers.
Shade in this picture by following the number key.

= 1
= 2
= 3
= 4
= 5

The scarlet macaw is one of the world's largest parrots. It can measure as much as 84 cm (33 in) from its beak to the tip of its tail.

Scarlet macaws are romantic birds. They have the same mate for life, raise their chicks together, and groom each other, too!

NAP TIME

Brown-throated sloths are known for sleeping a lot—about 15–18 hours per day! Guide this sloth through the maze so he can take a nap up his preferred tree.

Start

Finish

Brown-throated sloths can rotate their heads in nearly a full circle, like owls!

HELP OUT THE HERD

African elephants are larger and have bigger ears than Asian elephants.
African elephants have one dome shape on their heads, while Asian ones have two.
Each of these elephants has a twin, except one. Can you find the odd one out?

A wild elephant can live almost as long as an
average human. Its lifespan is around 60–70 years.

An elephant
can use its
trunk as a
snorkel!

FLOWER FINDING

Wildflowers grow all over the fields and hedgerows in Europe.
Look at the six sequences below. Can you spot them in the larger grid?

Dandelion   Daisy   Poppy   Primrose   Violet

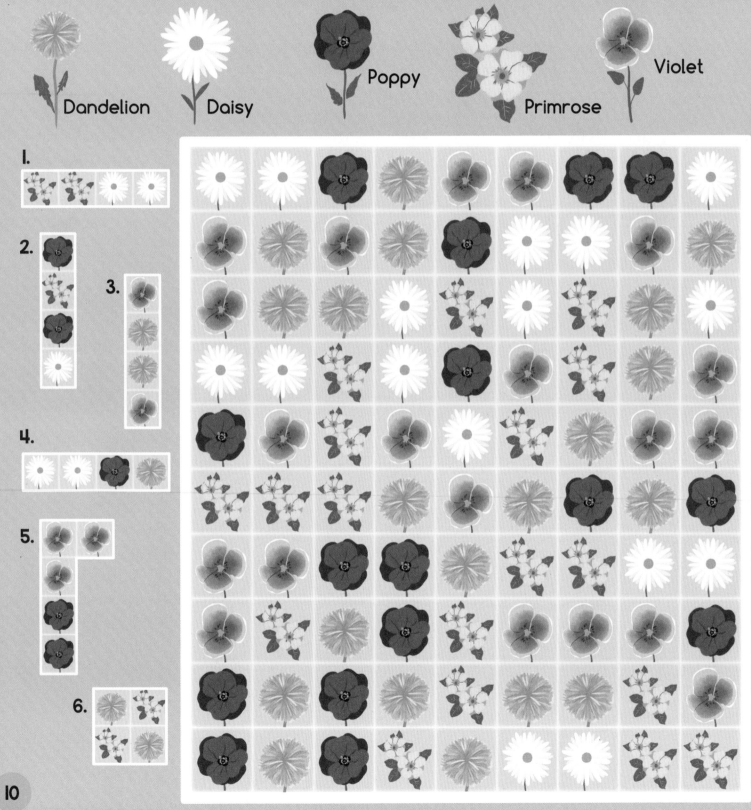

1.

2.

3.

4.

5.

6.

BUG HUNT

Insects and spiders are invertebrates—animals without backbones.
Read the clues and work out which creature is being described.

* It has a green body.
* It has fewer than eight legs.
* It does not have long wings.

June beetle

Caterpillar

Spider

There have been dragonflies on Earth for around 300 million years—since before the time of the dinosaurs!

Dragonfly

Ant

BAMBOO FOREST

Giant pandas are found high up in the mountains of a few regions in China. Take a look at the picture below, then see if you can spot all eight of the differences in the second image.

Pandas have some funny toilet habits. They sometimes pee while doing a handstand so they can spread their scent farther. Plus, they can poop up to 40 times a day!

ERUPTION DEDUCTION

There are about 1,500 active volcanos around the planet. Scientists define "active" as having erupted in the last 10,000 years! Read each fact below and check the box for true or false. Turn to page 88 to find out if you were right!

It is thought that the deadliest eruption—Mount Tambora, in 1815—killed about 1,000 people in the immediate aftermath.

T **F**

There is a type of bird that buries its eggs in the sand near a volcano to keep them warm.

T **F**

The word volcano comes from Vulcan— the Roman god of fire.

T **F**

The world's largest volcano is in Hawaii.

T **F**

There are volcanoes on Mars.

T **F**

Volcanoes can't be found under water.

T **F**

FALLEN LEAF

Follow the dots to finish off this picture of a leaf, then read the clues to discover which tree it belongs to.

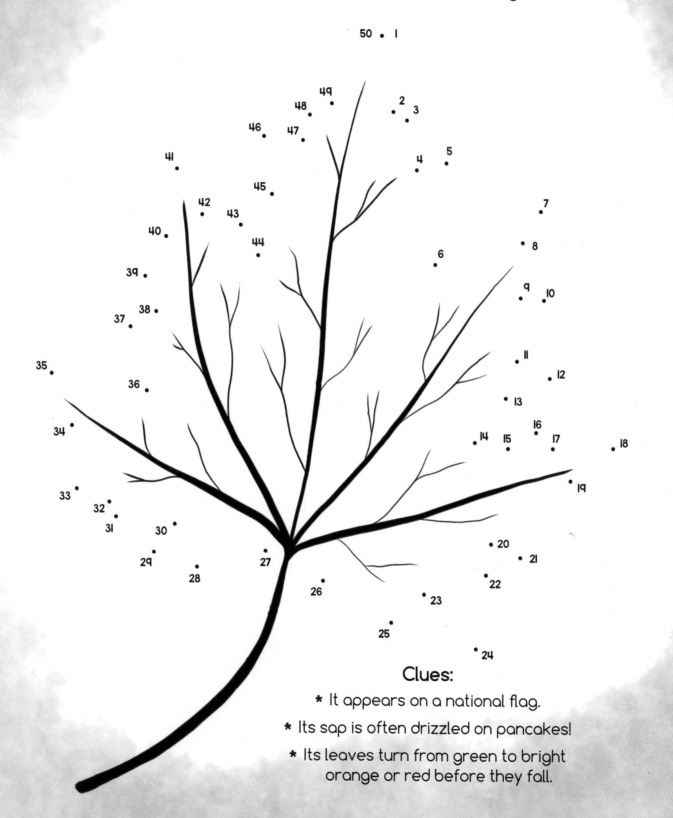

Clues:

* It appears on a national flag.

* Its sap is often drizzled on pancakes!

* Its leaves turn from green to bright orange or red before they fall.

HOW TO DRAW: A DOLPHIN!

Take a look at this picture of a bottlenose dolphin, then see
if you can copy it into the empty grid. Use the squares to help you!

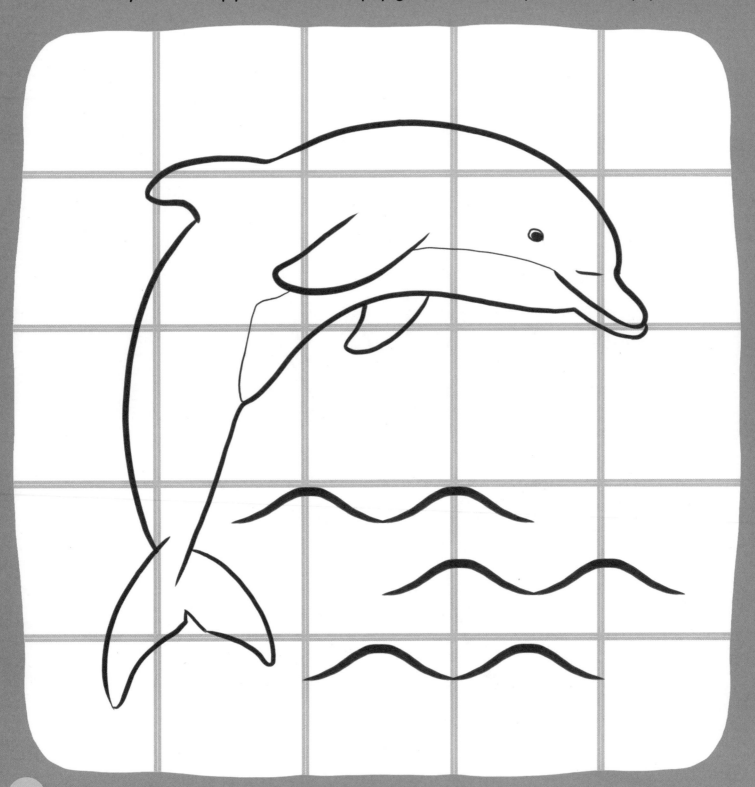

Bottlenose dolphins live in groups called "pods." They hunt, play, and raise young dolphins together.

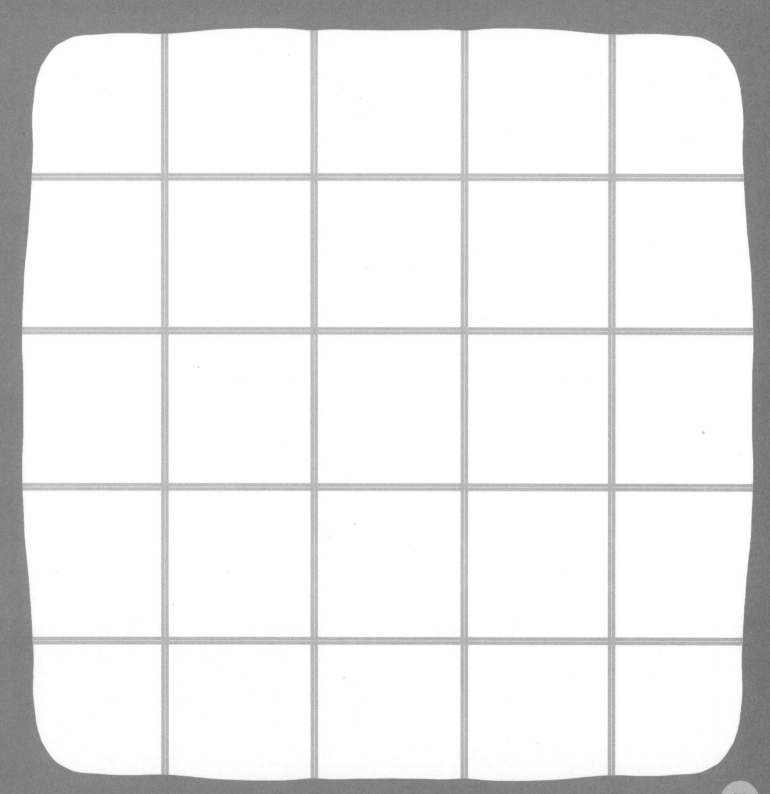

PATTERN MATCH

The pattern on a giraffe's coat is as unique as a fingerprint.
Look carefully and see if you can find which picture matches
the pattern on this giraffe.

Did you know that
giraffes don't need
much sleep? They only
doze for between
40 minutes and four
hours each day!

A

B

C

D

E

F

G

BABY LOVE

There's nothing cuter than a baby, right? How well do you know the names of these young animals? Rearrange the letters, then match each name to its picture.

AFLO

UCB

HTNCLAHIG

OJEY

EWLTO

Baby kangaroos are only 2.5 cm (just under 1 in) long when they are born. That's about the same size as a grape!

SWAMP ATTACK

Swamps are areas of land that are usually covered with water, and filled with trees and vegetation. They are the perfect home for alligators and crocodiles! Can you find three pieces of this picture that have been snapped off?

Alligators can live to 50 years old!

PEAK PUZZLE

Mount Everest is the world's highest peak above sea level. Use your number skills to work out how many days on average it takes to climb from the bottom to the top. Start with the top equation.

Mount Everest is 8,850 m (29,035 ft) tall. Researchers believe the mountain grows about 4 mm (1.57 in) each year!

Climbers may stop at different camps on their way up to the summit (top), to sleep and eat some food.

60 − 6 =

+

12 × 8 =

+

1,900 − 200 =

+

200 × 20 =

+

3 × 50 =

Mount Everest was formed over 60 million years ago! It happened when India's continental plate (piece of Earth's crust) collided with Asia's continental plate and pushed the land up.

TOTAL

÷ 100 =

number of days

SNOWY SCENE

These reindeer look right at home in the wintry Scottish Highlands. Take a look at these details and see if you can find and check off each one.

Reindeer grow new antlers
each year. Female reindeer
keep their antlers throughout
the winter while male reindeer
shed theirs in November.

AMAZING LIZARDS

Lizards have been roaming the planet for millions of years.
Can you match these lizards to the correct facts?

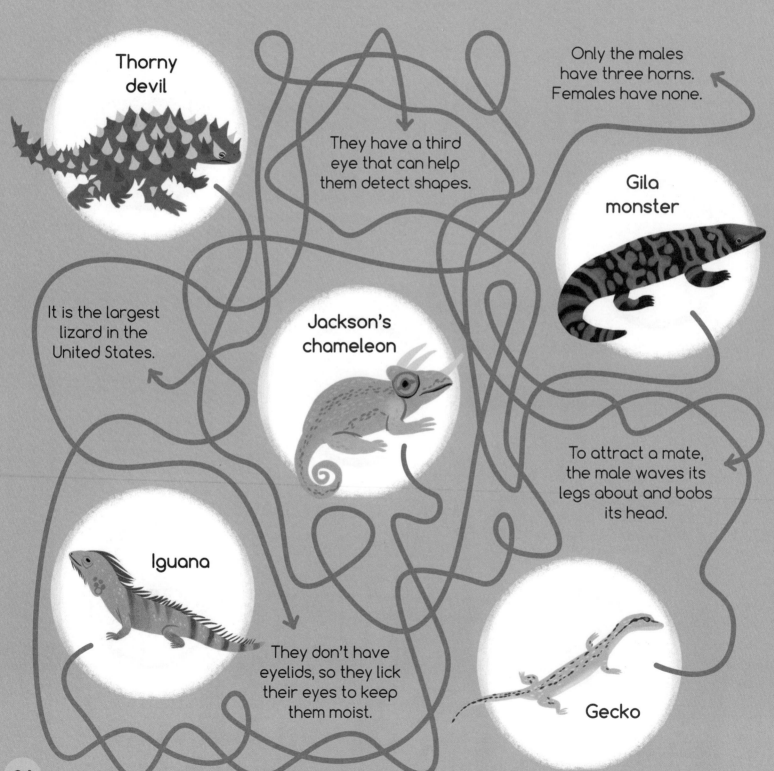

Thorny devil

Only the males have three horns. Females have none.

They have a third eye that can help them detect shapes.

Gila monster

It is the largest lizard in the United States.

Jackson's chameleon

To attract a mate, the male waves its legs about and bobs its head.

Iguana

They don't have eyelids, so they lick their eyes to keep them moist.

Gecko

FLUTTERING BUTTERFLIES

These schoolchildren have been visiting a butterfly farm full of amazing species. Take a look at the graph to see which butterflies they have spotted, then answer the questions.

Great Mormon swallowtail

Malachite butterfly

Christmas butterfly

Green-banded swallowtail

Forest queen butterfly

	Great Mormon	Green-banded	Christmas	Forest queen	Malachite
20					
18					
16					
14					
12					
10					
8					
6					
4					
2					

1. How many more forest queen butterflies were spotted than great Mormon swallowtails?

2. Which butterfly was spotted the least?

3. Which three species' totals, added together, would be more than the malachite total?

4. Which butterfly was spotted twice as many times as the green-banded swallowtail?

5. How many butterflies of all species were spotted in total?

25

FAMILY PRIDE

Can you help this lion cub choose the right path to find its family?

Like human babies, lion cubs are born without teeth. They get two sets during their lives—baby teeth and adult teeth.

Lion cubs are born with spotty fur. The spots disappear as they get older.

FOREST SUDOKU

Woods and forests are home to all sorts of animals, from birds and badgers, to rabbits and red squirrels. Fit each of these European woodland creatures into the grid. Each animal can only appear once in each row, column, and mini-grid.

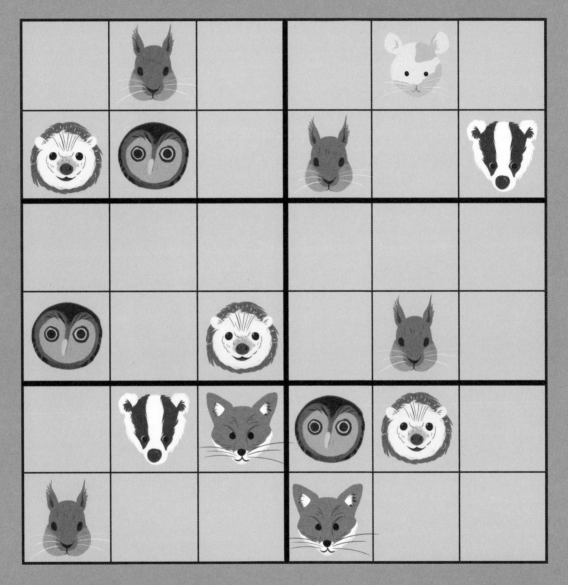

 Red fox
 Badger
 Mouse
 Hedgehog
 Red squirrel
 Tawny owl

PRIMATE PUZZLER

Use the code cracker to discover what each of these primates is called.

A	B	C	D	E	F	G	H	I	J	K	L	M	N	O	P
$	*	&	/	£	?	☺	@	§	«	🍎	♡	+	»	ɔ	=

Q	R	S	T	U	V	W	X	Y	Z	<	?	_	"	!	~
†	#	∞	‡	✈	•	€	‹	›	¢	¥	∞	©	∘	®	↕

The largest primate in the world is the eastern gorilla. It can grow to 1.88 m (6 ft 2 in) in height and weigh 204 kg (450 lb)!

☺ɔ#§♡♡$

ɔ#$»☺✈‡$»

♡£+✈#

*$*ɔɔ»

MOUNTAIN SHADOW

The Andes is a mountain range that covers almost the entire length of South America. Take a look at this picture, then see if you can find the exact matching silhouette below.

The Andes is the longest continental mountain range in the world, stretching from Venezuela to Chile.

A

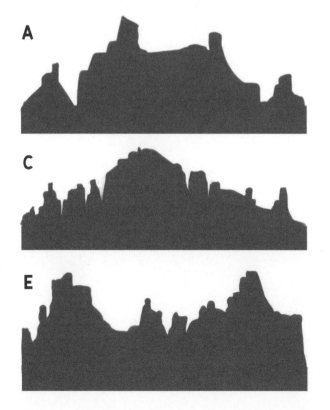

B

C

D

E

F

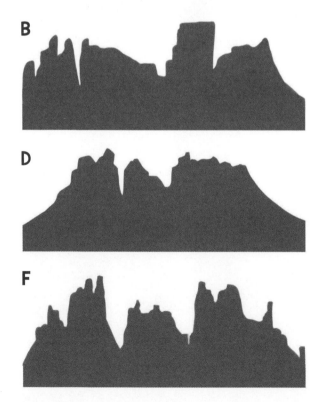

CLOUD SPOTTING

Read all about these different types of clouds, then see if you can spot which type is the odd one out. Pay particular attention to the clouds' positions in the sky.

Cirrus

The word "cirrus" comes from the Latin word for a lock or curl of hair—which is just what these wispy clouds look like! They lie high in the sky and look bright white in the day, but can appear orange at sunrise or sunset.

Cumulus

Cumulus clouds are round and puffy with bright white tops that appear darker at the bottom. They lie low in the sky.

Cumulonimbus

If you see cumulonimbus clouds, get ready for rain. They are usually low-lying clouds that stretch into the sky in high plumes.

Stratocumulus

These clouds lie low in the sky and are usually found in small groups, waves, or lines.

LOOKING LEOPARDS

Snow leopards have thick fur to keep them warm, and wide paws to help them walk across the snow. Can you draw lines to link the exact reflection of each snow leopard in the water?

Snow leopards are actually more closely related to tigers than leopards.

These big cats can't roar! Instead, they growl, mewl, purr, hiss, moan, and yowl.

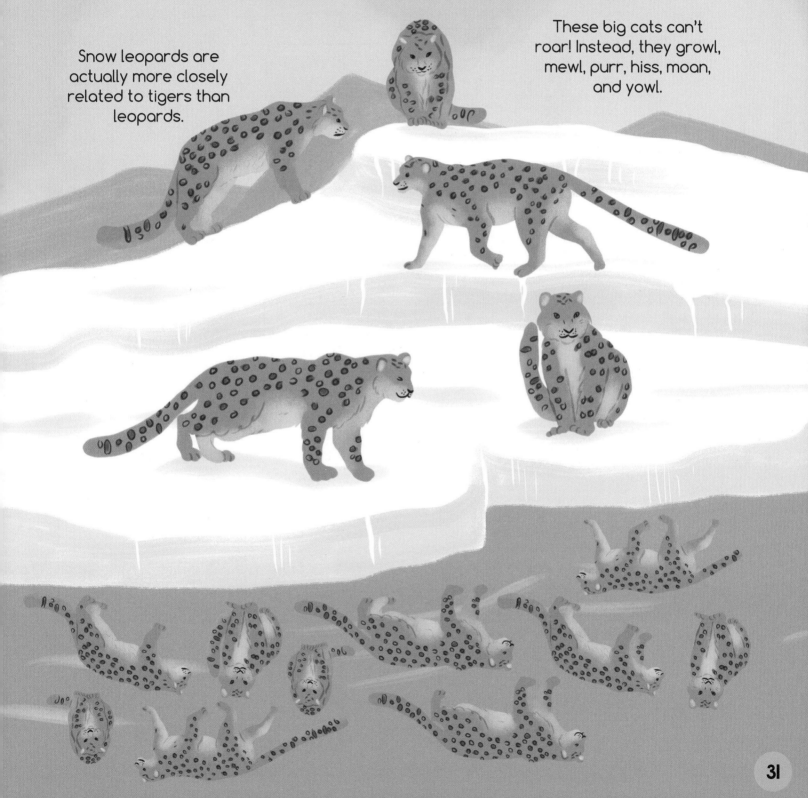

DESERT CROSSING

Camels are designed for long trips
across barren deserts like the Sahara.
They can store fat in their humps
and drink up to 114 l (30 gallons)
of water in one go.

Help this camel find its
way through the maze,
visiting each oasis
(place where water
is found) as it goes.

Start

Finish

POND DIPPING

Peek in a pond, and you'll see a wide variety of living things. Take a look at the picture below, then see if you can spot all eight of the differences in the second image.

Ponds are packed with life, both on and under the water!
Because they are quite shallow, plants can grow all across
the bottom—unlike many lakes, where plants only grow at
the edges, because it is too deep and dark in the middle.

FABULOUS FRUIT

Millions of creatures (including us humans!) eat fruit to keep fit and healthy. Can you find these sequences of fruits in the grid?

BIRDS OF PREY

Take a quick look at the picture below. Can you tell—without counting—
which bird appears the most often? Now check your answer!

Buzzard

Tawny owl

Goshawk

Red kite

TIGER TRAIL

There are six subspecies of tigers left in the world, many of which are endangered. Read about them, then draw the missing halves of the faces.

Indochinese tiger
These tigers are darker than other species and have narrower stripes. Their preferred habitat is forests and mountains.

Siberian tiger
These big cats are the largest subspecies of tiger in the world. They can survive in harsh conditions, such as the freezing snows of Siberia!

Bengal tiger
Large Bengal tigers can grow to up to 260 kg (573 lb). They live in the forests of India, Bangladesh, and a few other countries. White Bengal tigers are extremely rare.

South China tiger
South China tigers are critically endangered. Some scientists believe that all other tigers are derived from this first species.

Malayan tiger
Malaysia's national animal, the Malayan tiger is now critically endangered, with an estimated 150 left in the wild.

Sumatran tiger
These endangered tigers live in the forests of Sumatra. They are relatively small, and have orange fur and heavy black stripes.

Indochinese tiger

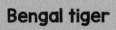
Bengal tiger

South China tiger

FLAMINGO TEASER

Take a look at these flamingos happily splashing about.
Count how many flamingos there are to start the puzzle,
then fill in the answers.

Start

A group of
flamingos, like the
ones below, is called
a "flamboyance."

Flamingos eat by
turning their heads
upside down and
filtering water
through their bills
to get to the good
stuff (such as algae
and shrimp).

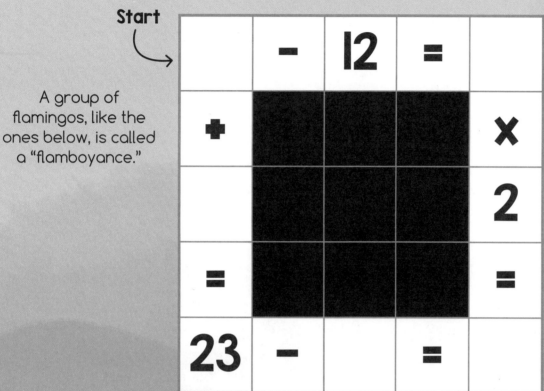

	−	12	=	
+	■	■	■	**×**
	■	■	■	**2**
=	■	■	■	**=**
23	**−**		**=**	

FACT OR FICTION?

Zebras are amazing animals. Read each fact below and check the box for true or false. Turn to page 91 to find out if you were right!

They can run at speeds of up to 32 km/h (20 mph).

T F

They can only be found living in the wild in Africa.

T F

Zebras only live to 20–25 years of age in the wild, but can live up to 40 years in captivity.

T F

They use a low grumble to warn predators to stay away.

T F

Foals stand up a day after being born.

T F

No one quite knows why zebras are black and white. It could be for camouflage, to keep them cool, or to confuse flies so they don't land on them!

Zebra's stripes are like fingerprints—they are unique to each zebra.

T F

RIVER RIDDLE

There are many major rivers on Earth, including the Amazon, Mekong, Nile, and Niger. Rearrange the letters to work out which are shown here.

Rivers only account for 0.49 percent of the Earth's water, but are vital for life on land.

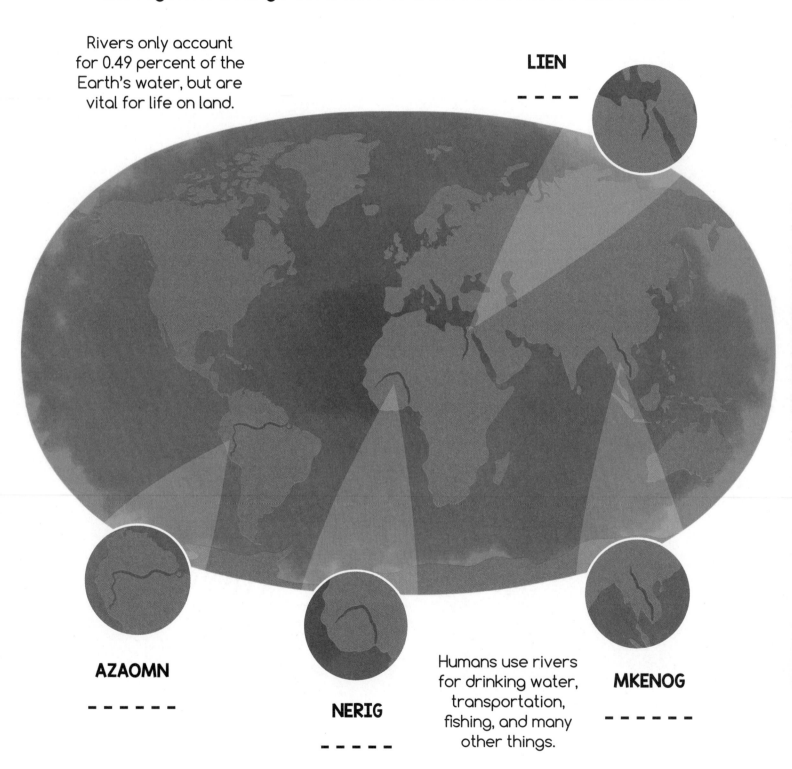

LIEN

_ _ _ _

AZAOMN

_ _ _ _ _ _

NERIG

_ _ _ _ _

Humans use rivers for drinking water, transportation, fishing, and many other things.

MKENOG

_ _ _ _ _ _

FLOWER MATCH

Follow the lines to match the flowers to the seeds or bulbs from which they grow.

Humans use seeds to grow plants. We also eat lots of different types—they're healthy as well as tasty!

CURIOUS CREATURE

Can you work out which animal this is? Follow the dots to find out, then shade in the picture with pens or pencils.

The height of this animal is measured using a unit called "hands."

This friendly animal can't breathe through its mouth! Air can only travel to the lungs when it is inhaled through the nose.

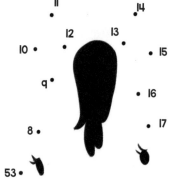
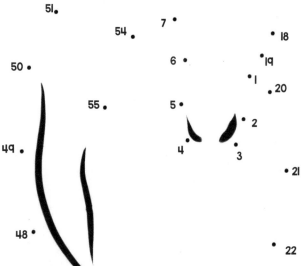
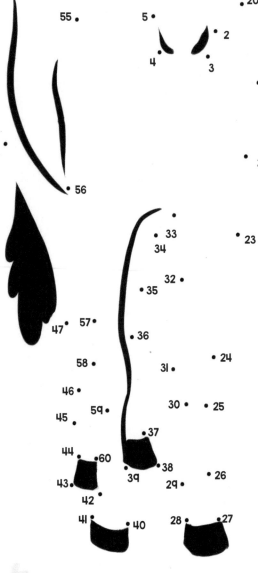

11
14
12 13
10 15
9 16
17
8
52 53
51
7 18
54
6 19
50 1 20
55 5
49 2
48 4 3
21
56 22
33 23
34
32
35
47 57 36 24
58 31
46 24
45 59 30 25
44 60 37
43 38 26
42 39 29
41 40 28 27

LAKE LINKS

Some people believe Lake Baikal in Russia is the deepest lake in the world. Take a look at this picture and see if you can find the missing pieces of the puzzle.

There is a myth that a strange animal lives in the depths of Lake Baikal. It is called Lusud-Khan, which means "Water Dragon Master."

TIME TO REFLECT

There are three species of zebra, all of which live in the wild in Africa. Can you work out which of the pictures below is this zebra's true mirror image?

Although many zebras live on grassy plains, some live in mountains and are excellent climbers!

Zebras sometimes live in mixed herds alongside giraffes and wildebeests.

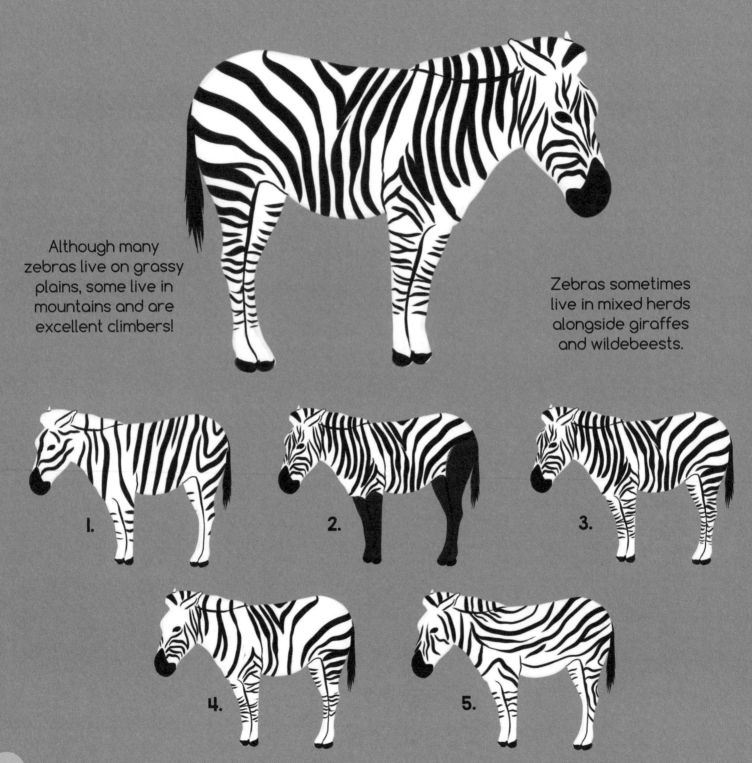

1.

2.

3.

4.

5.

ADDING-UP ANTS

Solve the equations to complete these ant-themed statements.

A black ant colony has between **A** and **B** female worker ants living inside.

An average black worker ant can live for up to **C** years.

Black worker ants can carry up to **D** times their own weight.

A $20 \times 20 \times 10$	**B** $10{,}000 - 3{,}000$
C $200 \div 100$	**D** $150 \div 3$

Black ants love sugary treats like rotting fruit!

NIGHT WATCH

Many different animals come out at night. Take a look at these details and see if you can find and check off each one.

Animals that are awake during the night are called nocturnal. Animals that are awake during the day (like you!) are called diurnal.

Wolves are the largest member of the dog family. They are the species from which pet dogs were domesticated thousands of years ago!

Raccoons are nocturnal animals that live in lots of different places—forests, prairies, marshes, and even cities!

THREE BEARS

Asiatic black bears are great at climbing. Take a look at the weights for each of the bears below, then examine the pictures and work out which tree is "bearing" the heaviest load!

Adult bear: 100 kg

Bear cub: 50 kg

Infant bear: 10 kg

Asiatic black bears have an amazing sense of smell, which makes up for their bad eyesight!

FEATHERED FRIENDS

Can you match the feathers to the birds they come from?

Pigeon

Swan

Dove

Peacock

Duck

Peacocks are the national bird of India. Only the males have bright blue bodies; females are mostly brown.

RAIN FOREST HIDE & SEEK

The rain forest is home to thousands of clever and creative creatures. Rather than hiding from predators, poison dart frogs want to be seen! Their bright markings warn larger animals to stay away. Circle and count the frogs in the picture.

CHASING WATERFALLS

Read these amazing facts about waterfalls, then see
if you can put this picture back into the correct order,
from top to bottom.

Niagara Falls, on the
border of the United
States and Canada,
is the most-visited
waterfall in the world.

Waterfalls "fall" into 10
different categories,
with names like plunge,
horsetail, or cascade,
depending on how water
flows through them.

Niagara Falls
is in two main
parts with an
island separating
them. The larger
one is called the
Horseshoe Falls,
and the other
one is called the
American Falls.

SNAKE TANGLE

How many snakes can you see slithering together?

Snakes use their tongues to sense their surroundings, which is why you see them poking out so often!

WEB WONDERS

The Darwin's bark spider makes the largest, strongest web of any spider. Take a look at the webs, below. Which one is the perfect match?

This spider's web can reach up to 2.8 sq m (3.3 sq yd) in size!

A

B

C

D

ANIMAL TRACKER

Different animals make different prints. Count each print below and write the numbers in the boxes, to work out which animal took the most steps.

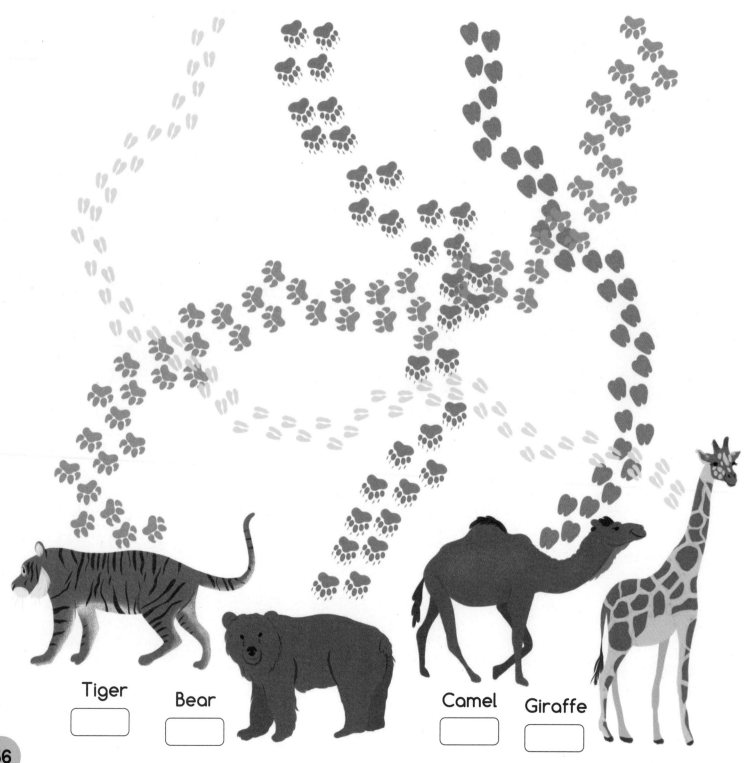

Tiger

Bear

Camel

Giraffe

THE LIFE OF A BUTTERFLY

Can you put these pictures of the lifecycle of a butterfly in the correct order?

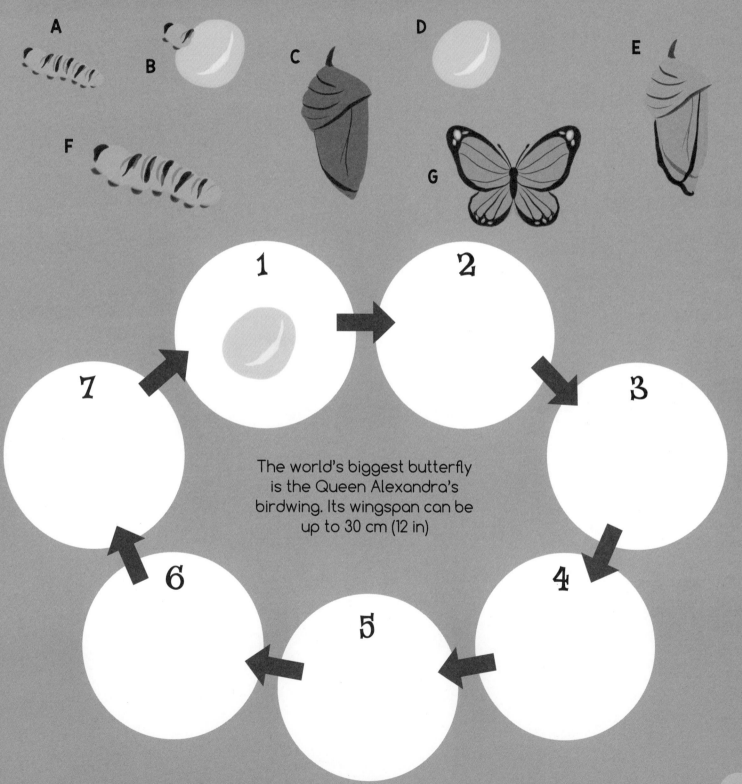

The world's biggest butterfly is the Queen Alexandra's birdwing. Its wingspan can be up to 30 cm (12 in)

ICE BREAKER

Antarctic pack ice forms during the winter, when surface water around Antarctica freezes into a layer of ice. Leopard seals rest on this ice when they take a break from hunting in the water.

Can you help this leopard seal to find its way through the ice?

Start

Leopard seals are the third largest seal in the world. They spend most of their lives alone—by choice!

Finish

SEASHELL SUDOKU

Look how these seashells have washed up on the shore. Can you complete the grid? Each picture should appear only once in each row, column, and mini-grid.

Scallop shell

Sea snail shell

Bivalve shell

Whorled shell

Seashells come in a huge range of shapes and sizes—nobody knows for sure exactly how many different types there are.

ALPACA FACT FILE

Alpacas are native to South America. Read each fact below and check the box for true or false. Turn to page 93 to find out if you were right!

They live to over 40 years of age.

T F

They are related to horses and are part of the equine family.

T F

An amazing 99 percent of the world's alpaca population can be found in South America.

T F

They are native to the rain forests of Brazil.

T F

Alpacas love to crunch on broccoli stems, apples, and carrots, but their main diet is grass, grains, and hay.

There are no wild alpacas—they are all domesticated.

T F

They hum when they are happy.

T F

RAIN FOREST RUSE

Rain forests are always full of life. Take a look at the picture below, then see if you can spot all eight of the differences in the second image.

In some parts of the forest, it can take as long as 10 minutes for a raindrop to fall from the top of a tree to the forest floor, because it has to travel down so many leaves and branches.

CLIMBING NUMBERS

The giant redwood is the one of the world's tallest types of tree. Climb to the top by filling in the missing numbers.

The number in each box is the sum of the numbers in the two touching boxes below it.

Redwoods wind their roots together with those of other redwood trees to help support each other when it gets windy.

Redwoods can grow to 116 m (380 ft) high.

The oldest giant redwood is believed to be over 2,200 years old!

64

GUINEA PIG MATCH-UP

Pet guinea pigs are bred in captivity, but they still have distant wild cousins in South America. Count the guinea pigs below—are there more with a pale stripe or ones that are a single shade?

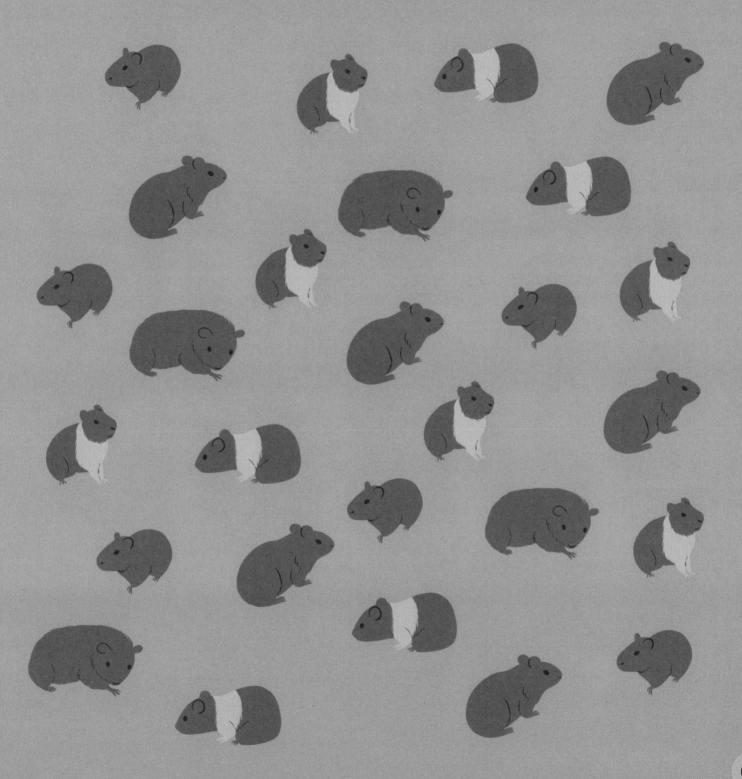

MEERKAT MAZE

Meerkats are very sociable. They can live in "mobs" of 40 members! Can you help this meerkat through the tunnels? You must visit each of the numbers and complete each mini-puzzle before moving on.

Meercats have strange tastes. In fact, one of their preferred snacks is scorpions!

Start

1. Unscramble the letters to find out where in the world meerkats live:

ROSTUEHN CFARAI

2. Solve the equation to learn how many years on average a meerkat lives for in the wild:

$56 \div 7 =$

3. If one meerkat eats 250 insects in one day, how many does it eat over an entire week?

3

Finish

STEPPING STONES

Precious stones like these take over a billion years to form.
Trace a path through the grid, following the pattern below.
You can move up, down, left, and right, but not diagonally.

Start

Finish

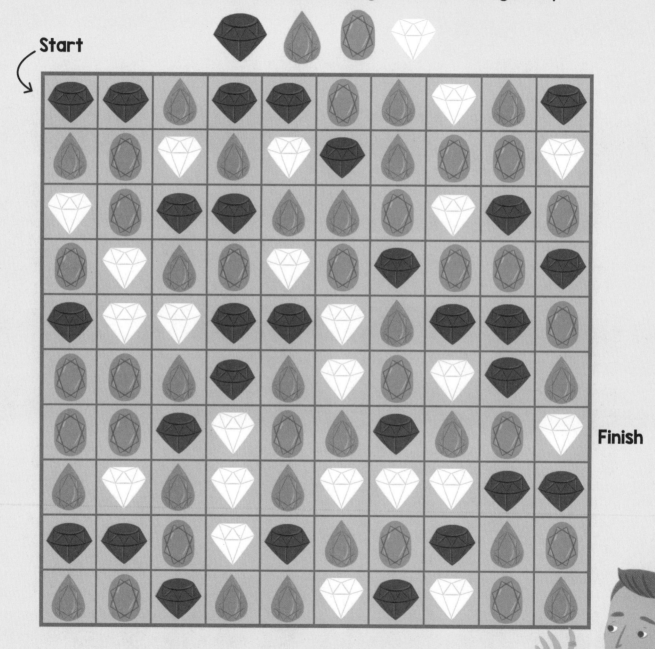

The largest diamond ever discovered was
called the Cullinan Diamond. It was originally
6 cm (2.5 in) wide and 10 cm (4 in) long but it
was cut up. Part of it is one of the UK's Crown
Jewels—a collection of precious treasures.

DIFFERENT DIETS

Herbivores are the vegetarians of the animal world as they only eat plants. Carnivores only eat meat. Omnivores eat both meat and plants. Can you sort these animals into their different categories?

CAPYBARA CASE FILE

Capybaras are the world's biggest rodents. Read each fact below and check the box for true or false. Turn to page 94 to find out if you were right! Then learn how to draw one step by step on the opposite page.

They have
webbed feet.
T ☐ F ☐

They are nocturnal.
T ☐ F ☐

Their teeth never
stop growing.
T ☐ F ☐

They live on their own.
T ☐ F ☐

They eat their own poop.
T ☐ F ☐

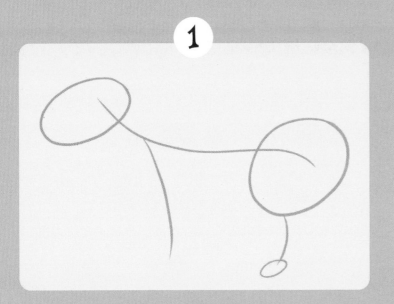

1

Draw an oval shape for the head and a circle for the bottom, as shown. Link these up with an elongated S to form a middle line. Draw in two lines to start the legs, and a back foot.

2

Add an eye, an ear, and a nose to the head, then draw curved lines as shown to create the back and stomach outlines. Now draw the front foot.

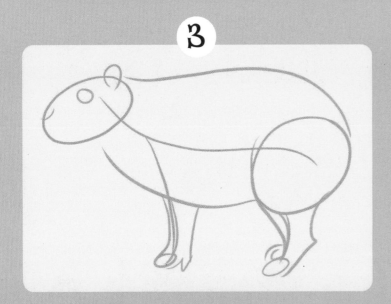

3

Use your leg lines to create stockier legs and feet. Remember to add in the bent back leg detail, as shown.

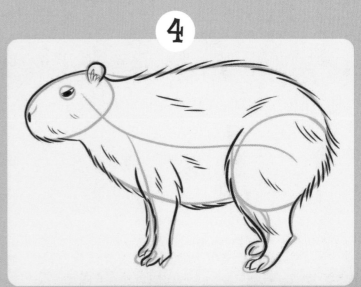

4

Once you are happy with your basic outline, rub out your guide lines and start to add in details, such as fur and toes.

PARK LIFE

This park in a city in China is teeming with life, despite being surrounded by skyscrapers! Have a look at these animals, then see if you can draw a line to the spot where they fit.

Plum Judy butterfly

Pallas's squirrel

Yellow-crested cockatoo

Turtle

BEING NOSEY!

Mandrills are recognizable thanks to their distinctive noses!
Follow the guide to shade in this mandrill's face.

They have large cheeks for storing food to snack on later in the day!

The mandrill is the world's largest monkey.

= 1

= 2

= 3

= 4

= 5

OCEAN DIVE

Ocean water covers 71 percent of Earth. Take a look beneath the waves and see if you can spot and check off all the things below.

Scientists estimate that over 80 percent of the ocean has yet to be observed or explored.

A blue whale can weigh as much as 40 elephants! It is the largest animal on Earth.

PEOPLE POWER

There are over 8 billion people on planet Earth. Where do they all live? Can you unscamble the letters to discover approximately how many people live in each continent.

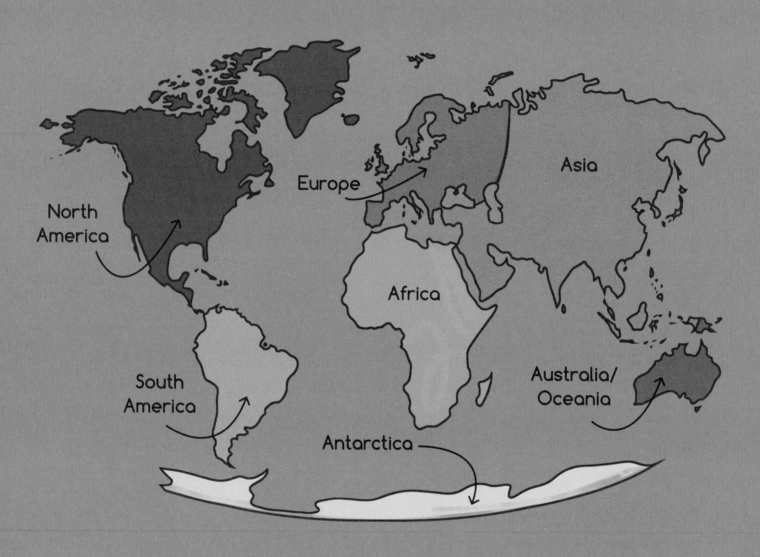

IASA =
4.7 billion

RCAATCINAT =
4,000–5,000 (in summer)

CAIARF =
1.4 billion

REPEUO =
748.7 million

RHONT EAICRMA =
374 million

ILSARAATU/ECNAOAI =
44 million

OHSTU RMCIAEA =
438.8 million

SPOT THE PILE!

Let's face it, living creatures produce a lot of poop! Follow the lines to see which pile of dung this rhino has made!

WALK ON THE WILD SIDE

The Black Forest in Germany is covered with evergreen trees, whose dark leaves give the forest its name. Guide these walkers along the paths from start to finish, collecting numbers along the way. The total target number is 20.

The walkers can only go along each path once, in one direction.

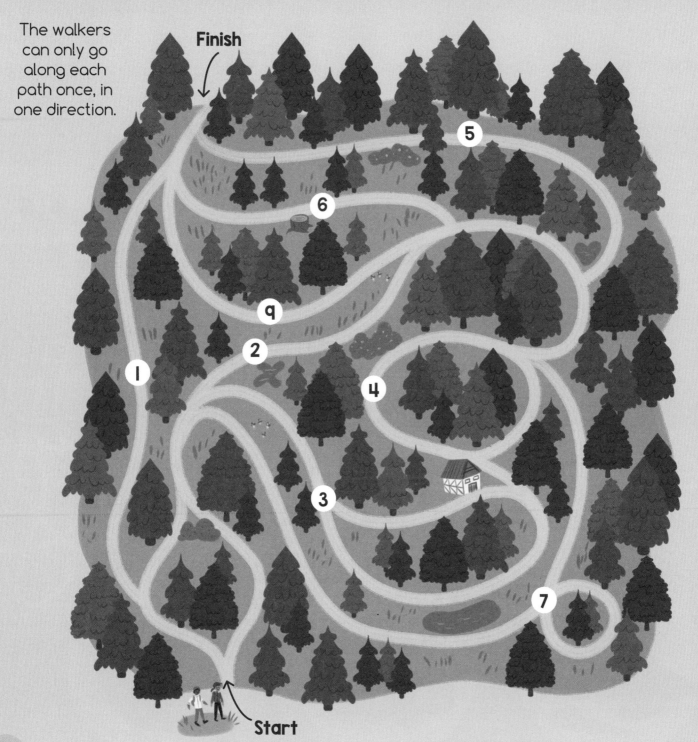

IT'S ELECTRIC!

Storms occur all over the world. Read the facts below,
then see if you can fill in the missing word from the list.

* What is lightning hotter than?

* How wide are lightning bolts?

* What country has more lightning strikes then anywhere else?

* True or false: It always has to be raining for lightning to strike?

* How far away can you hear thunder?

* How far away can you see lightning?

160 km (100 miles)

False

Venezuela

16–24 km (10–15 miles)

It's not true that lightning never strikes twice—it can strike the same spot lots of times!

The surface of the Sun

2-3 cm (0.8-1.2 in)

SAFETY IN NUMBERS

Many animals live for a surprisingly long time. Cross out the prime numbers in each of these groups. The number you are left with is the average age each animal can live to. Remember: A prime number is a number that can only be divided by 1 and itself.

Camels: 41, 43, 40, 47, 53, 59

Camels have three sets of eyelids, and two sets of eyelashes! This helps to keep sand and flies out of their eyes.

Wildebeests: 23, 20, 29, 17, 19, 11

Wildebeests can run at up to 80.5 km/h (50 mph).

Sloths: 7, 20, 11, 31, 37

Sloths are really strong. In fact, it's believed that they are three times stronger than a human!

Galápagos tortoises: 97, 100, 101, 109, 113, 89, 83, 127

Galápagos tortoises can go for up to a year without eating!

ARTY GARTER SNAKE!

Using the key, shade in this picture of the vibrant California red-sided garter snake. These snakes live near water, and are usually found in marshes and coastal dunes.

Garter snakes don't like to hibernate alone and will search until they find a community to hibernate with. These groups can often contain hundreds of snakes!

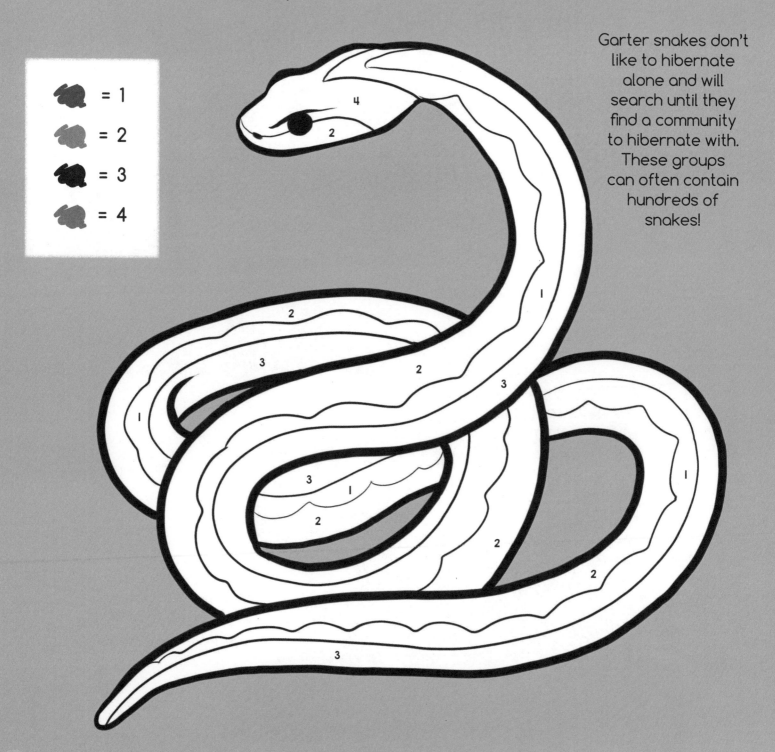

= 1
= 2
= 3
= 4

NATURE'S LIGHTSHOW

The aurora borealis are spectacular lights that can sometimes be seen in the skies near the poles. The beautiful natural lightshow has been captured in this picture—can you find the missing pieces?

The aurora borealis can be seen from the International Space Station.

QUESTION TIME!

What have you learned on your journey across the globe? Read the questions and see if you can discover the answers. Clue: You'll find everything you need in the pages of this book!

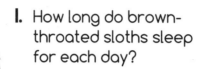

I. How long do brown-throated sloths sleep for each day?

a) 5–8 hours
b) 15–18 hours
c) 2–4 hours

2. How many times does a panda poop in a day?

a) 20
b) 30
c) 40

3. What is different about a lion cub's fur?

a) It has spots
b) It has stripes
c) It is white

4. What do you call an animal that is awake during the day?

a) Daytimmiul
b) Dalinial
c) Diurnal

5. Which country has the peacock as its national bird?

a) India
b) Canada
c) Australia

6. How old is the oldest giant redwood tree?

a) Over 220 years
b) Over 2,200 years
c) Over 22,000 years

7. What is special about the mandrill?

a) It is the world's largest monkey
b) It is the world's smallest monkey
c) It is the world's quietest animal

8. How long can a Galápagos tortoise go without eating?

a) Three months
b) Six months
c) Up to a year

HOW CAN YOU HELP PLANET EARTH?

Sadly, a lot of the animals featured in this book are endangered,
or close to being so. Take a look to see how you can help!

No palm oil!
Look for food and products that have a "no palm oil" or "palm oil free" logo. The harvesting of palm oil has led to the deforestation of some of the most important areas of the world, meaning that animals such as orangutans, elephants, and rhinos are at risk. The loss of these forests also contributes to climate change, since trees absorb carbon dioxide.

Reuse/recycle
Take a good look at what you throw away. Could it be saved? Could it be reused or recycled? When you are going on a trip, try to carry a reusable bottle and take all your trash home with you to be recycled, if possible.

Turn off the light!
If you are not using a room, make sure you turn off the light. This will avoid wasting precious energy.

Be a friend to wildlife
If you have some outdoor space, create a home for creatures. This could be a bug hotel or a patch of flowers that bees love to buzz around.

ANSWERS

Page 4
Spruce, pine, larch, and fir.

Page 5
There are 13 mangoes.

Page 6

Page 7

Page 8

Page 9

Page 10

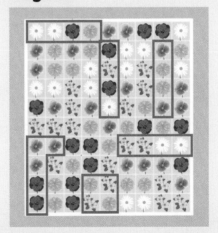

Page 11

It is a June beetle.

Pages 12-13

Page 14

These statements are false:

* It is thought that the deadliest eruption—
Mount Tambora, in 1815—killed about 1,000
people in the immediate aftermath.
**Historians think it killed about 10,000 people
in the immediate aftermath, and many more
after that, from secondary effects.**
* Volcanoes can't be found under water.
**Active volcanoes can be found on the ocean
floor.**

Page 15

It is a maple leaf.

Page 18

Page 19

 AFLO = FOAL

 UCB = CUB

 OJEY = JOEY

 HTNCLAHIG = HATCHLING

 EWLTO = OWLET

Page 20

Page 21

60 − 6 = 54

12 × 8 = 96

1,900 − 200 = 1,700

200 × 20 = 4,000

3 × 50 = 150

54 + 96 + 1,700 + 4,000 + 150 = 6,000

6,000 ÷ 100 = 60 days

Pages 22–23

Page 24

Thorny devil: To attract a mate, the male waves its legs about and bobs its head.

Gila monster: The largest lizard in the United States.

Jackson's chameleon: Only the males have three horns. Females have none.

Iguana: They have a third eye that can help them detect shapes.

Gecko: They don't have eyelids, so they lick their eyes to keep them moist.

Page 25

1. 8
2. Christmas butterfly
3. Green-banded swallowtail, forest queen butterfly, and great Mormon swallowtail
4. Forest queen
5. 44

Page 26

Page 27

Page 28

Gorilla

Orangutan

Lemur

Baboon

Page 29

Page 30

The odd one out is cirrus clouds as they are high-lying rather than low-lying in the sky.

Page 31

Pages 32–33

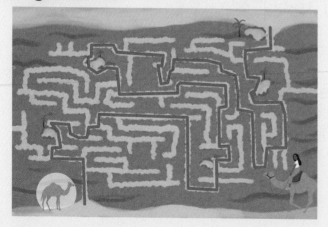

Pages 34–35

Page 36

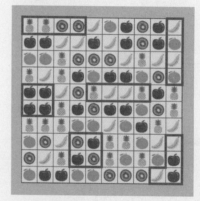

Page 37

Goshawks appear most often. There are 4 goshawks, 3 tawny owls, 3 red kites, and 2 buzzards.

Page 40

There are 20 flamingos.

20	–	12	=	8
+				×
3				2
=				=
23	–	7	=	16

Page 41

These statements are false:

* They can run at speeds of up to 32 km/h (20 mph). **They can run at speeds of up to 65 km/h (40 mph).**
* They use a low grumble to protect the herd from predators. **It is a high-pitched sound.**
* Foals stand up a day after being born. **It can be as little as six minutes!**

Page 42

LIEN = NILE
AZAOMN = AMAZON
NERIG = NIGER
MKENOG = MEKONG

Page 43

Dandelion seed

Sunflower seed

Poppy seeds

Daffodil bulb

Tulip bulb

Page 44

It is a horse.

Page 45

The missing pieces are E, D, and G.

Page 46

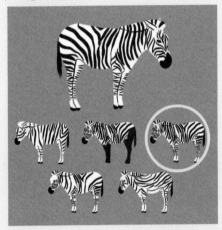

Page 47

A 20 x 20 x 10 = 4,000
B 10,000 − 3,000 = 7,000
C 200 ÷ 100 = 2
D 150 ÷ 3 = 50

Pages 48–49

Page 50

A Two adult bears = 200 kg
B One adult bear and one infant = 110 kg
C One adult bear, one cub, and one infant = 160 kg
D Three cubs = 150 kg

Page 51

Page 52

There are seven frogs.

Page 53

The correct order is 5, 4, 1, 3, 2.

Page 54

There are seven snakes.

Page 55

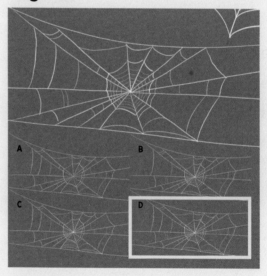

Page 56

Tiger = 53
Bear = 34
Camel = 36
Giraffe = 65
The giraffe took the most steps.

Page 57

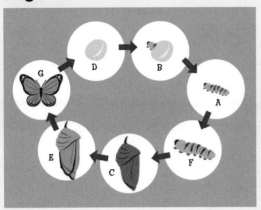

Pages 58–59

Page 60

Page 61

These statements are false:
* They are related to horses and are part of the equine family. **They are part of the camel family.**
* They live to over 40 years of age. **They live to 20 years of age on average.**
* They are native to the rain forests of Brazil. **They are actually native to the Andes mountains.**

Pages 62–63

Page 64

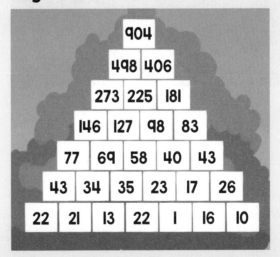

Page 65

There are 16 single-shade guinea pigs and 11 with a pale stripe.

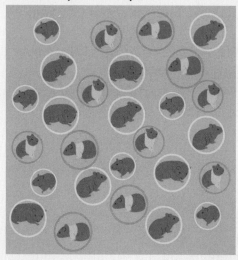

Pages 66–67

1. Meerkats live in southern Africa.
2. Eight years
3. 250 x 7 = 1,750

Page 68

Page 69

Herbivores: Zebra, giraffe, elephant
Carnivores: Tiger, lion, leopard
Omnivores: Hedgehog, meerkat, racoon, fox

Page 70

These statements are false:

* They live on their own. They live in groups.
* They are nocturnal. Their preferred time of day is dawn or dusk.

Page 72

Page 73

Page 77

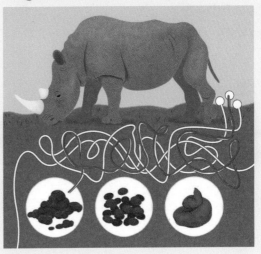

Pages 74–75

Page 76

Asia = 4.7 billion
Antarctica = 4,000–5,000 (in summer)
Africa = 1.4 billion
Europe = 748.7 million
North America = 374 million
Australia/Oceania = 44 million
South America = 438.8 million

Page 78

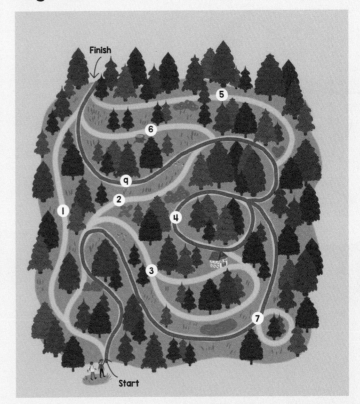

Page 79

* The surface of the Sun
* 2–3 cm (0.8–1.2 in)
* Venezuela
* False
* 16–24 km (10–15 miles)
* 160 km (100 miles)

Pages 80-81

Camels: 40
Wildebeests: 20
Sloths: 20
Galápagos tortoises: 100

Page 82

Page 83

The missing pieces are B, E, and G.

Pages 84-85

1. b) 15–18 hours
2. c) 40
3. a) It has spots
4. c) Diurnal
5. a) India
6. b) Over 2,200 years
7. a) It is the world's largest monkey
8. c) Up to a year